SEARCH
DINOSAURS

by Anne Cambal

PEARSON

Scott
Foresman

Editorial Offices: Glenview, Illinois • Parsippany, New Jersey • New York, New York
Sales Offices: Needham, Massachusetts • Duluth, Georgia • Glenview, Illinois
Coppell, Texas • Ontario, California • Mesa, Arizona

Every effort has been made to secure permission and provide appropriate credit for photographic material. The publisher deeply regrets any omission and pledges to correct errors called to its attention in subsequent editions.

Unless otherwise acknowledged, all photographs are the property of Scott Foresman, a division of Pearson Education.

Photo locators denoted as follows: Top (T), Center (C), Bottom (B), Left (L), Right (R), Background (Bkgd)

Opener: Corbis; 1 ©Joan Wiffen; 3 ©DK Images; 5 SuperStock; 6 Photo Researchers, Inc.; 7 British Library, Getty Images; 8 Corbis; 10 © Project Exploration P.A.S.T; 11 Corbis; 12 Corbis; 13 ©Joan Wiffen; 15 ©Joan Wiffen; 16 ©DK Images; 17 Corbis; 18 Corbis; 19 Corbis; 20 Corbis; 21 Corbis; 22 Corbis

ISBN: 0-328-1353 9-9

FASCINATING FOSSILS

Why do people like fossils? Fossils are a window into the past, a look at creatures that lived millions of years ago. Many of the plants and animals found in fossils are extinct. We'll never see them alive. For example, dinosaurs have been extinct for at least 65 million years. We only know about them from fossils.

Fossils are the remains of prehistoric plants and animals that have been preserved in stone. Fossils can be leaves, seashells, bones, or even footprints or bite marks. But while fossils are valuable for studying the past, they can be hard to find.

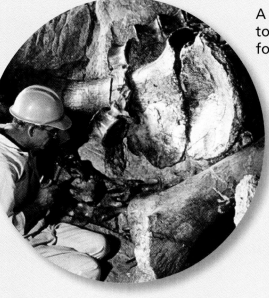

A scientist uses excavating tools to carefully remove fossils from rock.

Two of the tools used to excavate fossils

A DINOSAUR NAMED SUE

Fossils are most often found in remote areas where wind or rain exposes a few bones that hint at what is buried. The remoteness of some areas can make it hard to find and retrieve fossils. But curiosity drives fossil hunters to search wherever fossils are found.

Sue Hendrickson, a self-taught fossil hunter, has traveled all over the world in search of fossils. She has found fossilized whales in the desert of Peru and 24-million-year-old butterflies trapped in amber (fossilized tree sap) in the Dominican Republic. But her biggest discovery was made on a fossil dig in the United States.

In 1990, while searching in the Black Hills of South Dakota, Hendrickson found the fossil skeleton of a *Tyrannosaurus rex*. Named "Sue" in honor of its discoverer, it is the largest and most complete *Tyrannosaurus rex* yet found. Sue is believed to be about 67 million years old. It's estimated that Sue weighed seven tons when she was alive, and that her skull weighed six hundred pounds.

People have been finding fossils for hundreds, maybe thousands, of years. However, the first time a dinosaur fossil was scientifically described was about 200 years ago.

When was the last time you spent a day with a dinosaur? If you live in the Midwest, you can visit Sue at the Field Museum in Chicago, Illinois.

5

EARLY FOSSIL HUNTERS

Georges Cuvier developed the first system for classifying animals based on their anatomy, or body structure. He was a French scientist and zoologist who lived from 1769 to 1832. Cuvier also developed the science of paleontology.

Paleontology is the study of prehistoric life through the examination of fossils. It includes the study of Earth's layers, which are called *strata*. These layers help preserve fossils and provide clues to their age.

Georges Cuvier

Most scientists no longer use Cuvier's system of paleontology. However, Cuvier's ideas and studies helped greatly in making paleontology a respected science.

These bands of rock layers, or strata, might contain fossils.

Gideon Mantell, an English doctor who lived during the early 1800s, was one of the world's first paleontologists. He became interested in fossils as a teenager and corresponded with other early fossil collectors. They exchanged ideas and some of the fossils they found.

Dr. Gideon Mantell

Sir Richard Owen was nicknamed "the British Cuvier" for his work in zoology and paleontology. He lived from 1804 to 1892. In 1842 Owen first used the word *dinosauria*, from which "dinosaur" comes. *Dinosauria* is based on the Greek words for "terrible" and "lizard." Owen used the word to refer to a group of large, extinct reptiles.

Today, Mantell and Owen are known as the first people to identify and classify dinosaur fossils. They helped turn dinosaur paleontology into a major field of study.

Sir Richard Owen

In the early 1800s, one of the most active fossil hunters was a young woman named Mary Anning. Anning was from a poor family, but she had a passion for fossils. She made many important discoveries, and her fossils were bought by museums, scientists, and European collectors.

Barnum Brown began his career in 1897 at New York's Museum of Natural History. In 1902 he won fame for discovering the first *Tyrannosaurus rex* fossil. Brown worked as a paleontologist for sixty-six years, leading fossil hunts all over the world.

Brown's work marks the boundary between early and modern dinosaur paleontology. His discoveries greatly advanced the study of dinosaurs, but he lacked the modern equipment of today's paleontologists. Now let's look at the work of some modern dinosaur paleontologists.

Barnum Brown

STUDYING DINOSAURS TODAY

Today the field of dinosaur paleontology is thriving, thanks to the efforts of scientists worldwide. Modern communication instantly spreads news of each new discovery. It also makes it easier for dinosaur paleontologists to resolve disputes regarding how dinosaur fossils should be classified. Since the early 1800s, scientists on several continents have discovered more than three hundred species of dinosaurs!

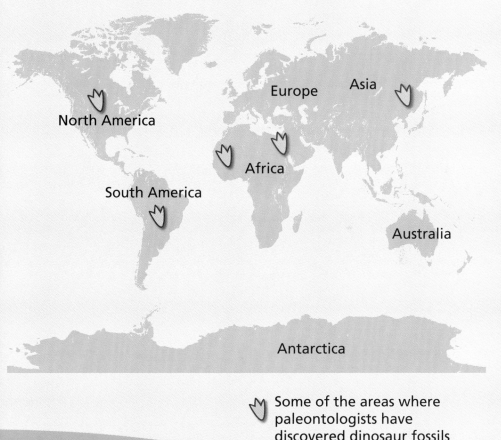

North America

Europe

Asia

Africa

South America

Australia

Antarctica

Some of the areas where paleontologists have discovered dinosaur fossils

A TEAM OF FOSSIL HUNTERS

Paul Sereno is a famous fossil hunter. While in college at Northern Illinois University, he was granted a behind-the-scenes tour of New York's Museum of Natural History. The museum's displays of dinosaur fossils fascinated him. Sereno was so impressed that he decided to study for a career in dinosaur paleontology.

Sereno worked hard to make his dream a reality. He studied collections of dinosaur fossils in China and Mongolia and earned a doctorate, or special degree, in geology from Columbia University. Sereno also married Gabrielle Lyon, a fellow paleontologist. Together, they became a team of great fossil hunters and have made many important discoveries in the field of dinosaur paleontology.

Paul Sereno

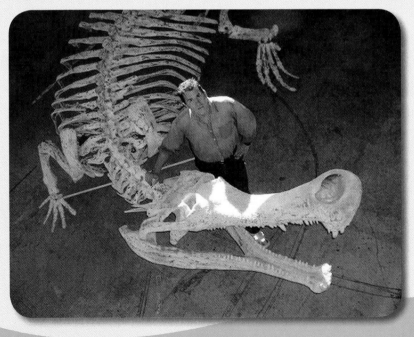

Scientists assembling a massive
fossil head of *Carcharodontosaurus*

In 1995 Sereno and Lyon led a fossil-hunting team
to Africa. The trip's highlight occurred when Sereno
discovered a fossil skull of a dinosaur species named
Carcharodontosaurus. Based on the skull, the team
estimated that a living *Carcharodontosaurus* would
have been forty-five feet long! Lyon also discovered a
new dinosaur fossil during the trip. Her find was named
Deltadromeus agilis, or "agile delta runner."

In 1997 Sereno was leading an expedition in the West
African country of Niger. David Varricchio, a member of
Sereno's team, spotted a fossil claw sticking out of the
desert sand. It was a great find, but even more lay in store.
Eventually, more than four hundred pieces of dinosaur
fossils were found scattered around the claw!

What Varricchio had found was a whole new species of dinosaur. It was named *Suchomimus*, which means "crocodile mimic." The skull of *Suchomimus* shows that it ate fish. *Suchomimus* was given its name because scientists believe that it ate like a crocodile.

People around the country were excited by the discovery of *Suchomimus*. It was mentioned on the front page of the *Chicago Tribune* and in *Time* magazine. *National Geographic* even gave the discovery its own television special!

Paul Sereno and Gabrielle Lyon are known primarily as fossil hunters. But they have done more than go digging around for fossils. In 1998 the couple cofounded Project Exploration. The organization has two main purposes. It tries to educate people about the latest discoveries in dinosaur paleontology. At the same time, it wants to get children interested in careers in science.

Claw from a *Suchomimus*

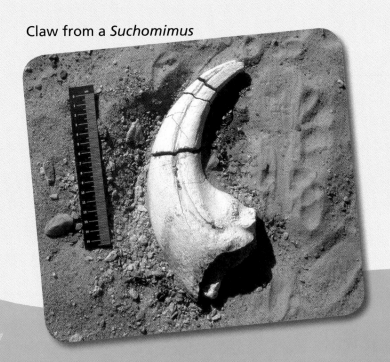

Joan Wiffen, the first person to find a dinosaur fossil in New Zealand, digs at an excavation site.

JOAN WIFFEN: AMAZING FOSSIL FINDER

Interest in fossil hunting is worldwide. Joan Wiffen is just one of many fossil hunters based outside of the United States. She specializes in fossil hunting in New Zealand.

Wiffen first became interested in dinosaurs when she read stories about them to her young children. It was an interest that suited her well. She was already an expert rock collector, having traveled around New Zealand for years looking for and identifying minerals and gemstones. During her rock-collecting trips, Wiffen gained a vast knowledge of New Zealand's landscape and geology. She also developed a scientific mindset and the keen eye of someone who spends her life hunting for objects buried in the ground.

On one **occasion** while out rock collecting, Wiffen bought a fossil of a trilobite, a small extinct marine animal, at a roadside stand. The trilobite made her even more interested in extinct animals. From then on Wiffen spent much of her time hunting for dinosaur fossils.

At first Wiffen had difficulty earning respect as a serious hunter of dinosaur fossils. The scientific community ignored her because she lacked a degree in paleontology. They also doubted that any fossils could ever be found in New Zealand, an island they thought was too small to have supported the huge prehistoric creatures.

Wiffen worked hard to prove the scientists wrong. She read tirelessly about fossils and dinosaur paleontology, studying the latest theories and discoveries. Her breakthrough came in 1974, when she found her first dinosaur fossil. It was the first ever found in New Zealand!

You have now read about some well-known dinosaur paleontologists and fossil hunters. Nowadays, some dinosaur paleontologists are involved in a new technology called animatronics. Keep reading to find out what animatronics is all about!

Joan Wiffen showed those who doubted that New Zealand had any dinosaur fossils that they were wrong.

MODERN VIEWS OF DINOSAURS: ANIMATION TO ANIMATRONICS

Anyone who has watched cartoon shows is familiar with animated cartoons. Cartoon animation was first developed as an art form during the early 1900s. It is similar to regular filmmaking. But while regular filmmakers film people or the natural world, animators film clay models, drawings, or computer images.

Computers have given a big boost to animation. They have also helped people develop animatronics, which combines animation and electronics. This technology is used to build robot models. Animatronics artists create electronic devices that make the body parts of their models move.

ANIMATRONICS VOCABULARY

animatronics, n.
A technology that uses electronics to animate or move puppets or other figures. Robotic models are designed to move at certain times. Dinosaur animatronics often include recordings of the sounds that scientists believe dinosaurs may have made.

animate, v.
To give life to or make something seem to be alive. In cartoons, the drawings seem to come to life.

animation, n.
The art or process of making animated cartoons.

Without computers it would be impossible to do modern animatronics. But animatronics is very different from the special effects that are made using computers. When computer artists create special effects, they use computer programs to draw images that you see later as part of a film. In many cases the special effects made by computers have made it unnecessary to build models.

In contrast, animatronics engineers create actual models. Animatronic models cost a lot of money and take many hours to design and build. Paleontologists, painters, sculptors, movers, technicians, and photographers must all work together in order to create realistic animatronic models. The following pages describe in detail how an animatronic model of a dinosaur actually gets made. Just turn the page to find out more!

An artist uses a computer to draw a blueprint for a new model of a dinosaur.

HOW TO MAKE AN ANIMATRONIC DINOSAUR

1. Make a drawing of the dinosaur model you have in mind.

2. Build a miniature model using the drawing as a guide.

3. Sculpt a full-sized model using the miniature model as a guide.

4. Make a **mold** from the full-sized model. Pour the material used to make the skin of the finished dinosaur into the mold.

5. Design and make the parts that will control the model's animatronics.

6. Combine the molded figure with the animatronics to create the finished product.

7. Test everything to make sure it works!

1. Make a Drawing

First, an artist draws a sketch of the dinosaur. The sketch is much smaller than the animatronics model that will be built from it. The artist may study fossils of the dinosaur. He or she will pay close attention to individual parts, such as the hands or head, but will make sure that all the parts are in **proportion** in the finished drawing.

The initial drawing serves as the **foundation** for the work that follows. It must be done as accurately and completely as possible, because all the other steps are based on it.

2. Build a Miniature Model

The artist then makes a small model, so that everyone can see how the dinosaur will look from various angles. The model also helps determine whether the original drawing of the dinosaur can actually be transformed into an animatronics model.

3. Sculpt a Full-Sized Model

The finished miniature model serves as the basis for the full-sized model. Sometimes the full-sized model is created by hand. Other times it is built using a process called CAM, which stands for **C**omputer-**A**ssisted **M**anufacturing. Any marks or flaws in the finished full-sized model must be **tidied** up before the final details are carved onto its surface.

4. Make a Mold and Cast the Figure

Once the full-sized model is complete, artists use it to make a mold for the final product. Since the final model is usually very large, it is often molded in several smaller sections. These sections must fit together perfectly for everything to work. At this step the machinery that controls the final model is placed inside the mold. This is done to make sure that the machinery will fit properly into what will become the final model.

An artist assembles a cast of a dinosaur head.

Engineers test the machinery that controls the movements of a dinosaur model.

5. Make the Parts for the Animatronics

At the same time that the molds are made, the animatronics machinery that controls the final model's movements is designed and built. Four different types of systems are used to create the internal workings of the dinosaur. These systems are called the mechanical, structural, surface, and electronic systems. They work together to move the dinosaur's head and jaws. They also support the weight of the figure each time its body or tail moves. The systems also make the skin look realistic and coordinate things so that the dinosaur model moves in a lifelike way.

6. Assemble It All

Once work on the molded figure and its animatronics is complete, everything is assembled and tested. As each new part of the dinosaur model's frame is connected, its machinery and fit are also tested. By testing each section while it's being assembled, problems can be identified and fixed before it is too late.

7. Test, Test, and Retest

Once the entire dinosaur model has been **erected,** the final stage of testing begins. The purpose of these tests is to make sure that all the systems work, that the dinosaur figure will hold together, and that the color and texture of the dinosaur will look good on film or on display. During testing the dinosaur remains in the **workshop,** where the equipment and materials are available for making changes.

After the dinosaur model has passed the tests, it is moved from its workshop to a new location, where it either becomes part of a museum exhibit or is filmed in a movie or television show. This process usually requires the use of cranes and trucks. Obviously, none of the scientists, artists, or engineers involved in building the model have ever seen a living dinosaur. But they've done their best to create the best possible model for the museumgoers or moviegoers to see, hear, and enjoy!

Workers assembling a full size model of a *Tyrannosaurus rex*

Glossary

erected *v.* built; set up.

foundation *n.* base; part on which other parts rest.

mold *n.* a hollow shape into which soft or liquid material is poured and that gives its shape to the hardened material.

occasion *n.* particular time.

proportion *n.* a proper relation among parts.

tidied *v.* to have put in order; to have made neat.

workshop *n.* a building or area where work is done.